BASIC FOREX SUPPORT
AND RESISTANCE

Learn the basic of support and resistance and how to
effectively identify them

Abraham Robert. C

In order to say thank you for purchasing this book, I offer the below video course and more to you as a token of appreciation

**Find the Link to the bonus video courses at the end of the book**

TABLE CONTENT

CHAPTER 1

Understanding Support and Resistance

Similar to any other trading market, supply and demand influence the price of financial assets. Support and resistance levels serve as an accurate representation of how supply and demand interact to set the current price of an underlying asset in financial markets.

Prices typically increase until supply exceeds demand, which is the resistance point at which they begin to decline. In a similar vein, prices will decline until supply cannot keep up with demand; at that moment, prices will begin to rise.

Purchasing an asset when prices are at a support level and selling it when prices are at a resistance level is the fundamental trading approach.

It is crucial to remember that support and resistance levels are areas where supply and demand might fluctuate rather than precise price points.

Market players keep a careful eye on levels of support and resistance because they are all eager to seize any chances that present themselves when supply or demand shifts.

Understanding how asset prices normally move is the first step in using support and resistance successfully. From there, you can interpret support and resistance using that framework. It's also important to understand that there are many degrees of resistance and support, such as minor and major/strong. Strong levels are more likely to hold and drive the price in the opposite direction than minor ones, which are predicted to be broken.

CHAPTER 2

TYPE OF SUPPORT AND RESISTANCE

The market offers a wide variety of support and resistance lines. Their formation process distinguishes them. Some of the most crucial levels that each trader should be aware of are included in the list below.

Horizontal Support and Resistance

The most fundamental kind of these levels is horizontal support and resistance. All that's needed to identify them is a horizontal line. The first step is to identify a previous price level that the price struggled to break above or below. Next, draw a horizontal line that extends into the future to indicate it. There's a good likelihood the price will retrace from this horizontal line as it reaches it once more.

Horizontal Resistance

Horizontal Support

Round-Number Support and Resistance Levels

Round-number levels are a different kind of support and resistance level that arises around round-number exchange rates. These psychological levels correspond to resistance and support.

There are more market orders near round numbers because players in the market typically place their stop levels or profit objectives around such levels.

Vertical Support and Resistance

Instead of using horizontal lines to represent support and resistance levels, trendlines—which can slope either upward or downward—are used. Trendlines are frequently used to detect uptrends and downtrends in the Forex market since it is a trending market.

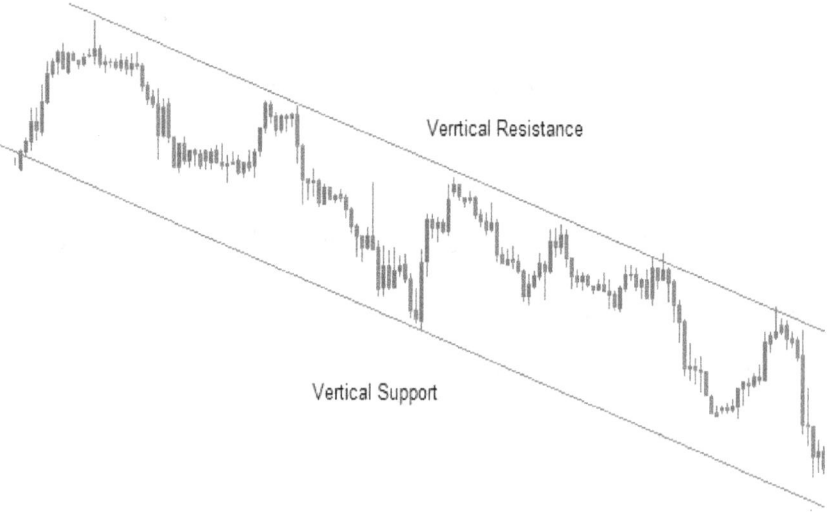

There is a good probability that the price will bounce off a trendline whenever it gets close to one.

Similar to horizontal levels of support and resistance, the trendline must have at least three price contacts in order to be deemed significant.

Fibonacci Levels Support and Resistance

One of the most often utilized tools for determining potential ending points for a market drop is the Fibonacci retracement. The underlying tendency so continues as a result. Price corrections, which give price charts their distinctive zig-zag shape, are countertrend price movements that occur during uptrends and downtrends. Fibonacci Levels of Support and Resistance.

One of the most often utilized tools for determining potential ending points for a market drop is the Fibonacci retracement. The underlying tendency so continues as a result.

Price corrections, which give price charts their distinctive zig-zag shape, are countertrend price movements that occur during uptrends and downtrends.

There are two applications for the Fibonacci indicator: When a moving market is retracing, Fibonacci retracements assist traders in determining the best entry positions, while Fibonacci extensions assist traders in determining the trending market's most advantageous goal points.

Fibonacci retracement lines will function as resistance lines in a decline and as support lines in an upswing. Fibonacci extension lines, on the other hand, will function as support lines in a downturn and resistance lines in an upswing.

Fixed Support and Resistance area

These are the constant, unchangeable levels of support and resistance. They won't become void until prices break through either above or below them. Fixed support and resistance levels include psychological and emotive levels like round numbers or significant past price points like all-time highs and lows.

Round figures, like $100, for example, can act as support or resistance for the price of an item in the market. However, prices like $2,000 for they might be seen as a level of support or resistance.

Dynamic Support and Resistance area

These levels of support and resistance, as their name implies, fluctuate in tandem with changes in both price and time. These levels suggest that as time and price change, new supply and demand dynamics, like as and, will affect prices and provide dynamic support and resistance levels.

Semi-Dynamic areas of Resistance and Support

Support and resistance levels that are semi-dynamic fluctuate with time and price, but they do so at a set or predefined pace. Trendlines, and are a few of the indicators that plot semi-dynamic support and resistance lines. These indicators show lines of support and resistance that systematically shift over time in response to changes in price.

A support level is a price at which there may be more demand that is, purchasing pressure for the financial instrument being tracked. Support levels are often past swing lows in the market, but they may also be price levels found on technical indicators like Fibonacci levels, trendlines, and channels.

In a nutshell, support levels are those that the price previously attempted to go above but failed to do so.

As a result, these price points are probably going to be viewed by technical traders and other market players as potential areas of renewed demand for the instrument.

Pivot Points

Several lines that act as levels of support and resistance in the market are mathematically derived by the Pivot Points indicator using the open, high, low, and closing prices.

Seven lines are shown by the indicator: three support lines (S1, S2, and S3), three resistance lines (R1, R2, and R3), and one pivot point (PP). A support line becomes a resistance line when it is crossed, and vice versa. For example, the line will now function as support if there is an upswing and the asset price crosses R1.

CHAPTER 3

Identifying the level of resistance and support

To determine the amounts of support and resistance, there are several methods. These levels are very simple to identify, but they may be quite helpful in determining when it's best to enter a market and where to place your stops and limitations. Traders can use the following to determine levels of support and resistance:

Past pricing information

Historical prices are an excellent resource for traders since they are the most dependable source for determining support and resistance levels. It's important to get familiar with historical patterns, perhaps from relatively recent behavior, so you can identify them if they recur.

It's crucial to keep in mind, though, that historical patterns can have developed in diverse contexts, making them not necessarily a trustworthy indication.

Previous support and resistance levels

As indications of future movement as well as potential entry and departure locations, you might utilize previously significant levels of support or resistance. It's crucial to remember that significant levels of support and opposition are rarely exact numbers.

It's probably more helpful to think of them as support or resistance zones because it's rare for a market to repeatedly hit the same price before reversing.

Technical indicators

Dynamic support or resistance levels that shift as the chart develops can be found using technical indicators or trendlines.

It might take some time to become proficient at identifying the support and resistance levels that will affect a market's price because these levels are frequently dependent on various reasons for different markets. Because of this, it's critical to practice utilizing previous charts to determine levels of support or resistance.

Chart Patterns

In addition, borders of support and resistance on charts prevent the price from breaking past the pattern. For example, triangles are made up of two lines that frame the triangle: a lower line that acts as support and an upper line that acts as resistance.

The price is not allowed to break above or below these lines until a particular momentum occurs, at which point bulls or bears are prepared to take control of the market.

CHAPTER 4

How to Draw Support and Resistance Lines

We need to have at least one pricing point where we may set our horizontal line in order to construct horizontal support and resistance lines. Typically, that price point is recognized as a clear swing high or swing low where the price has already reversed course.

Support and resistance lines must first be identified on a chart using one of the following techniques:

- ✓ Highs and lows
- ✓ Support and resistance levels from a previous timeframe
- ✓ Moving averages
- ✓ Trend lines

Highs and lows

Choose your timeframe, locate the highest peak on the chart, and then repeat the process to construct your lines using peaks and troughs. Write the highs and lows of each. The lower-high peak will be the resistance level and the lower-low peak will be the support level in the event of a downtrend. On the other hand, in the event of an upward trend, the higher-high peak would represent resistance and the higher-low peak would represent support.

Support and resistance levels from a previous timeframe

If you're going to be using support and resistance levels from a prior period, pick a brief one, like fifteen minutes. Next, depict the levels on the 15-minute frame from the one-hour and four-hour time frames. Strong levels of support and resistance may be present if the levels from the larger time frames are substantially comparable to or equal to the levels from the shorter time period.

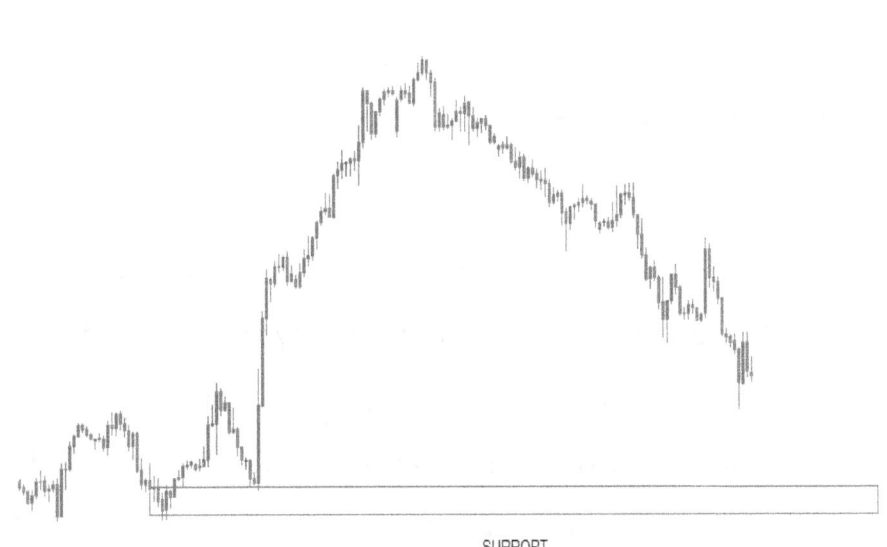

SUPPORT

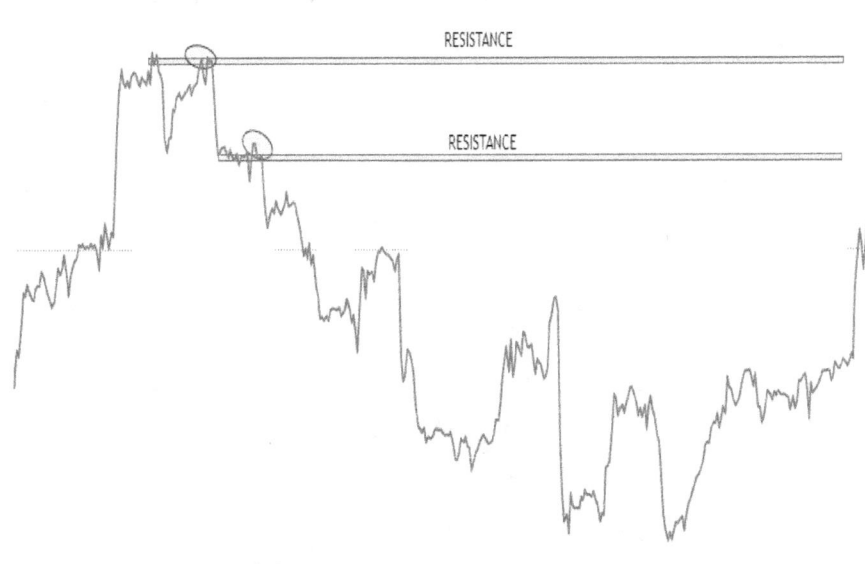

RESISTANCE

RESISTANCE

Moving averages

Another tool for determining and charting support and resistance levels is the moving average indicator. To determine which way the trend is moving, draw a diagonal line from the highest peak to the lowest peak while the indicator is activated. This moving average line will serve as a level of support if the trendline rises upward, and vice versa. The reason for calling this dynamic support or resistance is the ever-changing levels.

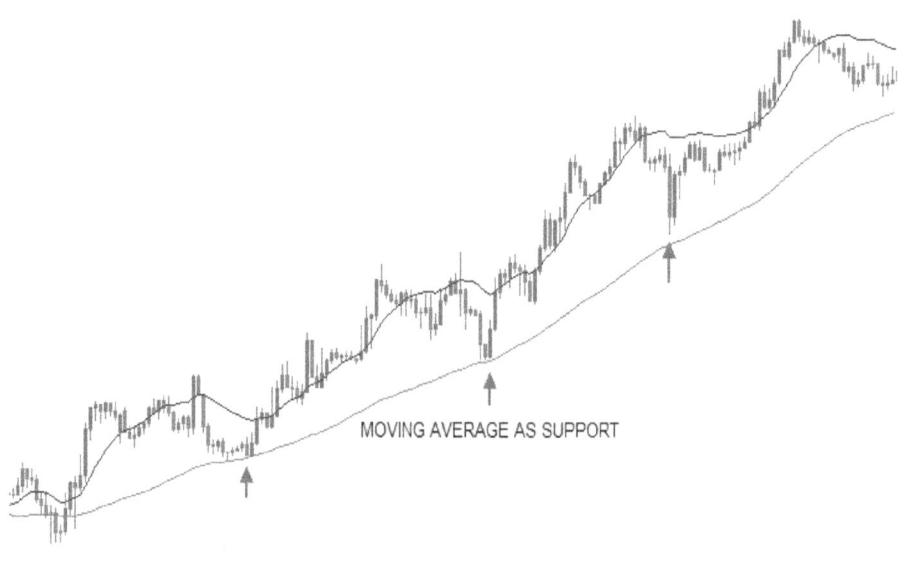

MOVING AVERAGE AS SUPPORT

Moving Average Acting as Resistance

Trend lines

In order to create a trend line that may be used, make sure you have at least three peaks or three troughs before drawing your lines. Your uptrend line will then be the support level and your downward trend line will be the resistance level once you've placed the trendlines into your chart.

These levels are dynamic, just as moving average support and resistance levels.

To determine the most precise support and resistance levels, it is crucial to combine one or more of the aforementioned techniques.

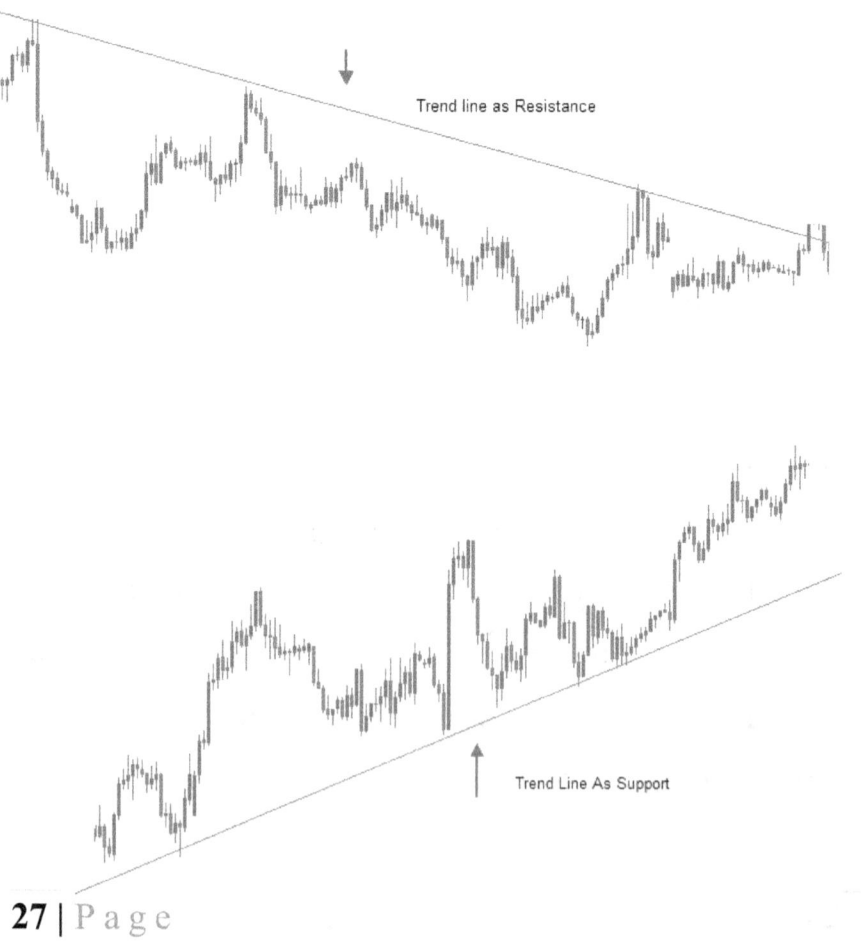

Trend line as Resistance

Trend Line As Support

Trendlines serve as the basis for and are beneficial to traders. A trendline is drawn from a single low in an uptrend, linking subsequent higher lows and extending the line into the future. The line then serves as a support line that is semi-dynamic.

A trendline is created from a single high in a downtrend, linking succeeding lower highs and extending the line into the future. The line then functions as a resistance line that is semi-dynamic.

You need at least two contact points where the price has bounced in order to construct a line. These are the highs or lows that are shown on the graph. A line will be observed as a major level by more traders the more touch points it has.

The majority might not consider a line with only two points of contact, or if these are not true bounces, in which case the line breaking might not have a significant effect.

Certain product lines have the ability to endure for many years and continue to be in demand even though the majority of market players today did not help create them initially. When you chart lengthier time frames, get ready to spot lines from the 1980s and 90s!

Since they highlight the primary obstacles, longer time horizons provide an excellent view on the most relevant S and R levels. To obtain more precise levels, however, you still need to perform the same on shorter time frames.

CHAPTER 5

SUMMARY

In technical analysis, support and resistance levels are among the most crucial components for creating profitable trading strategies.

Support and resistance, however, are much more than simply some lines on a chart when you understand them well. Gaining sustained profitability requires the ability to identify particular pricing points that drive price patterns.

A price chart's support and resistance levels show supply and demand graphically. When supply and demand are balanced, prices will essentially stay within a predetermined range

The floor price is indicated at the bottom of the bandwidth. This is the price at which the disputed commodity is in high demand; enough purchasers are prepared to pay that amount for the shares. "Support" is the term used to describe this lowest pricing.

Because more sellers desire to get rid of their goods at this price, demand stops and supply rises to the upper side, which represents the peak price. "Resistance" is the name given to this highest price.

The established levels of support and resistance will act as a barrier where there is a minimal likelihood of the price falling sharply below the bottom price or rising over the top price, provided that supply and demand continue to be in balance.

But certain things can cause a sharp shift in supply and demand. For instance, the firm may share good news that unexpectedly boosts demand to a much higher level, rendering the current levels of support and resistance meaningless.

Support

a price point, region, or zone where we anticipate higher buyer demand, supporting the price level and halting future price declines.

Resistance

A price level, region, or zone where we anticipate higher seller supply, providing resistance to the price level and halting future price increases.

Remember that we are discussing a pricing range, region, or zone. Seldom does support or resistance exist at a single price point. Before deciding on a final course, the price will frequently go above and below a certain support or resistance level.

For further and advance knowledge on support and resistance get volume 2 of this book from amazon store.

Title: Advance Forex Support and Resistance.

GET INSTANT ACCESS TO THE FREE VIDEO
COURSE BY FOLLOWING THE BELOW LINK

subscribepage.io/freeforexcourse

Click or copy and paste the above link on your browser
for instant access to the bonus video course.

Best!

www.ingramcontent.com/pod-product-compliance
Lightning Source LLC
Chambersburg PA
CBHW072226290526
45794CB00007B/2901